Praise for *The Light on Sifnos*

Winner of the 2020 Blue Light Press Poetry Prize

Barbara Quick is a novelist of international reputation, and her skills are evident here, with characters we can believe; an atmosphere we can feel; and interior thoughts that deepen her observation. Every poem is a small story with personality and purpose— lines that flow like silk, holding words precise in every note. Quick gives us an island where we can go whenever we want to make beauty our own and rest in the company of flawless writing. Poetry has good reason to celebrate today.

— Grace Cavalieri, Maryland Poet Laureate

"Praise the wisdom of the wanderers / who kiss the earth, at last / returning home," Barbara Quick tells us in the final poem of *The Light on Sifnos*, and the reader feels satisfied with the rightness of the ending for such a beautifully rendered journey through light and dark, time and timelessness. In poems written as she read Emily Wilson's new translation of Homer's *Odyssey*, Quick's language is as lyrical as it is accessible. While her dead are as vividly present as the living, her keen awareness of mortality doesn't interfere with the giddy release from the quotidian that travel can bring, as when she plunges naked into the Aegean to join her "selkie mate." There's deep joy in these poems. There's also deep wisdom, fully deserving of praise.

— Lynne Knight, author of *The Language of Forgetting*

The haunting power of this collection is not epic, but Sapphic: mysteries rising from a handful of fragments gleaming in the sun. Barbara Quick's Sifnos is a place of elemental beauty, alive with the Attic past, peopled with the ghosts still living, still wandering with the other shades in the poet's soul as she navigates her way (with her father's old compass) through this world, "the future home of all we are and all we dream / in gleaming transit through the dark."

— George Bilgere, author of *Haywire*

Infused with some of the characters and themes from *The Odyssey*, Quick does a wonderful job weaving together the ancient tale with modern-day Sifnos. The narrative is compelling, informed, indeed, by the light on Sifnos that seems to lend a transparency to the poet's observations about life on the island and her own journey. *The Light on Sifnos* is a book you'll want to read many times so you can fully absorb its beauty and richness.

— Stewart Florsheim, author of *A Split Second of Light*

In the arc of this book, the poet arrives at a Greek Island and stays where "the shadows are as deep as wells, the air as clear as something newly born." There she burrows into the stony layers, paying attention to how the place reveals itself—its loneliness, its fullness, its fires, its sounds, its humor, its people living and dead. The poems, beautifully crafted and written in a voice that one instinctively trusts, celebrate the miracles of both travel and arrival. They radiate a sense of pilgrimage made with others, the epic journeys we all embark upon, and they praise with Homer "the wisdom of the wanderers."

— Mary Kay Rummel, former poet laureate of Ventura County, California, and author of *Nocturnes: Between Flesh and Stone*

Barbara Quick has set her poetic odyssey against a background of Greek landscape, history, and myth, yet her poems are always well-observed and intimate. We meet the island's car-washer, waiters, and a street-sweeper, who is "like the wind that rakes the air clean." Her own ghosts flicker in and out: mother, father, sister, a dear friend's son. The light on Sifnos reveals "rocky slopes that seem to hold/ the dead inside them," but also places where "shadows are as deep as wells, the air as clear/ as something newly born." This book is a small gem.

— Jeanne Wagner, author of *Everything Turns into Something Else*

THE LIGHT ON SIFNOS

Poems by
Barbara Quick

written on the Greek Island of Sifnos
while reading Emily Wilson's new translation
of *The Odyssey*

BLUE LIGHT PRESS ✦ 1ST WORLD PUBLISHING

SAN FRANCISCO ✦ FAIRFIELD ✦ DELHI

Winner of the 2020 Blue Light Press Poetry Prize
The Light on Sifnos

BLUE LIGHT PRESS
www.bluelightpress.com
bluelightpress@aol.com

1ST WORLD PUBLISHING
PO Box 2211
Fairfield, IA 52556
www.1stworldpublishing.com

BOOK & COVER DESIGN
Melanie Gendron
melaniegendron999@gmail.com

COVER ART
The Light on Sifnos by Brooks Anderson
BrooksAndersonArt.com

INTERIOR ILLUSTRATIONS
Melanie Gendron

AUTHOR COVER PHOTO
Laurie Bell Bishop
LaurieB.photography

INTERIOR PHOTOS
Wayne Roden

FIRST EDITION

ISBN: 978-1-4218-3697-3

for Wayne Roden,
my partner on the pilgrims' road

Table of Contents

The Light on Sifnos

How does one describe the light here in this place
where the dawn really does have rosy fingers,
where the mountains glow at night,
their barren slopes a magnet
for the radiance of moon and stars,

Where white-washed houses on the lowest slopes
are strung like chalky pearls
around the mountain's throat,

And oleander blossoms burn like hot pink coals?
The shadows are as deep as wells, the air as clear
as something newly born.

Even early morning light burns its mark
on tender human skin, as if the sun were reaching down
to tell us that we're changing
as surely as the plants that bloom and fade,
each bright blossom's moment
giving way to new ones.

The ferry comes and goes many times every day,
bringing bright new tourists to the island,
taking others away.

What News Awaits Us Here?

Athena spoke to Telemachus
with words that flew like birds.
Guided by the goddess, Telemachus
left home to seek news of his father.

Were we guided by a goddess
to leave our fertile home —
the vineyard lush with grapes,
my garden pushing out fruit —
to journey to this distant, rocky place?
What news awaits us here?

The Bread My Mother Gave Me

She apologized that it was
probably stale — but how could it not be,
when handed to me
in a dream, on a visit
from the Afterlife?

It had honey baked into the middle
and was more delicious
than any bread
I'd ever tasted.

I told her how grateful I felt
for this sustenance from her,
however late it came —
for the loving way she looked at me
across that distance
between life and death,

A hand's breadth between us
as I received
that holy bread
and ate to fill
that hungry place
inside me.

My Father's Maritime Compass

I didn't realize, when I packed it,
that it wasn't meant to find one's way on land.
Point it at a lighthouse. Point it at the Pole Star.
If you'd taught me how to use it,
I could journey through the starry nights
by sea, like Odysseus,
with fifty strong men at the oars and
a goddess watching over me.

I would stand there at the helm,
once again your cherished child,
face tipped upward, eyes focused
on the luff of the sail.
Flush with your approval for my light touch
with the tiller, I'd point us into the wind
as close as I could
without causing us to jibe.

You taught me how to crew,
to wait until that moment when the jib went slack
and then pull swiftly on the line,
hand over hand, ending in a final tug,
my feet in white-soled sneakers
braced against the combing of the cockpit.
Wind the jib-sheet round the winch
and make it fast, cinched between the teeth
of the cam cleat. Shove the heavy handle in,
and ratchet clockwise, while I
or someone stronger tailed the line.

Some things, it's true, you taught me well —
but how to find my way in life and love
was not among these.

I wish you had your compass with you now
as you journey through the darkness
with the other shades, maybe here
on this island, in the starlight,
on the naked rocky slopes that seem to hold
the dead inside them, glowing at night
with all they loved and hoped for,
all they lost and all they failed to find.

Christos, Who Collects the Trash

Slight of build, dark-haired
and always unprotective of his smile,
he is the happiest man in Kamares
or maybe anywhere on Earth.

He knows that what he does is good —
the village is a nicer place because of him.
Along the single, one-lane road, along the beach,
he picks up any trash he finds

And puts it where it won't offend our eyes.
He's like the wind that rakes the air clean.
He loves his job and loves his life —
such dignified contentment I've never seen.

"Kalimera!"— Good morning! — he calls out to every passer-by,
his skin baked brown, his mustache neatly trimmed.
I think his mother must have loved him well —
he glows with the goodness such love confers.

Was she alone in life? Was he the gift
that someone left behind, someone who arrived on the ferry
and left, never to return, never to know
that she bore his child and named him Christos?

"Kalimera!" he says to everyone he meets,
his dark eyes bright, his head held high.

Cicadas Sing the Poet's Ancient Words

The shepherds call their sheep and goats
with sounds as old as these rocky, god-strewn slopes,
where shade is gold and feed is scarce.

The only plants that thrive are those
well-schooled in deadly arts:
hot-pink oleander with its toxic blooms,
thistles as perilous to ruminants or human legs
as Bronze Age spears.

Everything with its strategy
to stay alive.

The only green, the wild thyme —
purple blossoms, fragrant leaves
preserved by ancient gods
to flavor mortals' offerings.

Cicadas launch the same cascade of sound
as heard by Homer as he sat, unseeing,
reciting the six-footed lines of the Iliad
and Odyssey, committing them to memory,
knowing they were gifts to him from the gods.

Cicadas saved the sounds of ancient Greek
and passed them down from century to century.
Flexing and unflexing the jointed tymbals
of their hollow bodies,
emerging from their years spent underground
as nymphs, to sing at last and find a mate
and reproduce and die.

Like poets, they leave a shell of themselves
behind: delicate, transparent,
redolent of rhyme.

The Mad Car-Washer of Kamares

Across the way from our cottage, half-hidden
by a wall, he shouts and sprays the rental cars
his boss drives over from the port. His head is bare,
his gray hair long, his face and neck a mask of scars.
He handles the high-pressure hose
as if it were a weapon and he a warrior.

Did his forbears live on the mountainside
that's backdrop to his labor, their brown arms
wielding bronze to make the rock give up its gold?

Apollo Rental Cars seems anything but old
and yet the madman they employ
evokes the ghosts of Ancient Greece:
hard-muscled men whose arguments still echo
in the valley, whose joys were brief and violent,
whose only comforts were women, drink and sleep —
or maybe sheep. It probably didn't matter much to them.

What kind of life is this, washing tourists' dusty cars
all day, explosively, compulsively — angrily —
one at a time?

The boss, Apollo, is pale-skinned
and tall, his beard as neatly trimmed as that
of any immortal god. He drives too fast
down our one-lane road. They shout at one another.
It sounds as if they'll come to blows.

The ferry brings more tourists to the island.
Apollo picks them up in bright and shiny cars.

The Farmer-Owner at His Bistro

The farmer's arms embrace
two baskets of tomatoes
clutched tight to his big, shambling frame,
making him look like a pregnant bear.

Small, bright-red and sound, they gleam
in the rose-tinged air as he pours them out
onto the green shelf set like a shrine
in the restaurant patio
with its westward view
and distant sound
of lapping sea.

The waiter, an elegant fellow,
stands by to catch tomatoes that stray
as the farmer constructs his still-life,
topped by an artful bouquet
of rosemary.

The sea is seeping inland, underground,
as ever more tourists discover the island,
bringing life-giving custom,
flushing more toilets,
taking more showers,
drawing the aquifers down.

Soon the island's water will be too salty
to grow the crops the farmer loves like children,
the perfect fruits of his labor
on display above the bistro's little garden
of culinary herbs.

The cook's assistant crouches there,
choosing with care the sprigs of sage and thyme
for the evening's lamb or goat *mastello*.

Old Men on Their Motorbikes

I love the old men on their motorbikes,
looking so happy,
as if they've stolen
years they thought were lost to them —
cheated death
in a last, mad, joyful
dash for freedom
on a narrow, perilous
one-lane road.

The Poem My Sister Might Have Written Here

So glad to see the moon again
this morning, above the mountain.
She kept watch while I slept,
rising full and butter-yellow
like a loving sister.
A nightlight while I slept.

I didn't fear the dark when she was there,
in loco parentis — standing in
for both our parents' love
in different ways.

My big sister lit the darkness
in the room we shared.
Sang me endless Irish ballads
till I fell asleep, transported by those stories
from long ago.

And then she left when I was eight years old.
Left me in darkness on the mountain
to find my way by starlight,
barefoot on the heartless rocks,
without a song or story,
with no one there
to watch me fall asleep
and keep me safe.

The Pilgrims' Road

Who can guide us on this journey,
up this rock-strewn mountainside
studded with thistles and thorns?

Who will guide us down again,
on the final leg of our passage
in the moonless dark?

How will we manage, when it's so hard now,
both of us still strong enough
to walk the pilgrims' road
with all the others, young and old,
their faces tinged with rosy light?

How can we fill our hearts with hope
when we harbor no illusions of a light-filled god
who'll hold us when we stumble through that final,
backlit passageway, all substance of self dissolving
in the ocean of sky?

The Gods Play Tricks Here

On the seaside terrace
of the taverna
run by one large family,
a gust of wind lifts
all the paper napkins
tucked beneath
the baskets of bread on the tables.
Up they fly, like decks of cards,
like flocks of birds, up in the air
and then
down into the sea.
Messages for Poseidon
from Hermes?

Another night,
at the restaurant next-door,
three waves rise of a sudden
from the placid sea
and crash over the terrace,
drenching diners,
making tourists flee.

Skinny-Dipping in Vathy

Above the azure inlet of the sea,
the path was steep, carved out between
the thistles, thorns and wind-blown rock.

He left her at the top to find a sheltered place
they wouldn't be seen descending to the shore.
She waited, fully clothed there,
till, looking down, she saw his gleaming skin
and upturned face above the churning deep,
as if he'd changed from man to seal
and loved this transformation.

She shed her clothes and picked her way
as far down as she could on tender feet —
then took a leap of faith, exchanging rock
for empty air, a rush of cold and bubbles
in her hair. Her toes touched seaweed
as she swam toward her selkie mate.

Two naked, slippery people,
seventy and sixty-five,
feeling so alive and filled with joy,
treading water side by side in the extra-salty,
turquoise blue Aegean Sea, rich in iodine,
with the power to heal
all kinds of wounds.

They tasted salt and kissed,
two shipwrecked sailors
who'd managed to survive.

The Bus to Apollonia

I saw you on a bus,
on the road to Apollonia —
thirty-five years younger
than you are now.

You looked right through me.
I wanted to cry out with joy,
"Jude! It's me!"

But I was in the present
and you were in this island's crazy time zone,
where those we've lost
sit laughing at cafes
or searching through the mountains
in the moonlight.

I wanted to protect you
from the sorrow in your future —
from the senseless murder
of the newly minted man
who was your darling son.
But I couldn't reach you.

If I see Jordan here,
among the other shades,
I'll tell him to look for you
on the bus to Apollonia,
at just the age you were
when he was a baby.

I know you love him well enough
to break the rules of time,

to find him on this island,
and hold tight and never let him reach
that dark street or that terrible night.

Meteor Shower

A denser brew of darkness as we walk,
blindly, down the pathway into night.
Heads craned back, we fill our eyes
with stars that start to fall from blackest skies —
moments too brief to register as real
and yet they pierce the heart
like all the greatest works of art.
Each glittering trail of light festoons the night
and feeds an appetite for more.

And more stars fall and, sore of neck,
we lay ourselves upon the ground
to contemplate the burning space debris
more comfortably.
Our still-warm selves the topmost skin
of all the layers of all that lived and now decays:
The future home of all we are and all we dream
in gleaming transit through the dark.
The earth that will replace our breath
and know the final number of our days.

The Feeling of Earth on My Fingers

Sometimes I like to take the gloves off —
to pull the weeds and gather the harvest
bare-handed. To remember this is earth,
not dirt. To keep my body's memory
fresh — here where the roots twine down,
searching for sustenance. Here
where the worms create their magic:
this will be my bed. A flowerbed,
perhaps. A vegetable garden
blushing with its own abundance.

These plants, all of them, are wiser
than I will ever be. They know
how to drink the mist and make the most
of every photon of sunlight
and moonlight, too, living ever
in their moment of life.

Praise the wisdom of the wanderers
who kiss the earth, at last
returning home.

Acknowledgments

"The Feeling of Earth on My Fingers," "Meteor Shower," and "Skinny-Dipping in Vathy" were published on *YourDailyPoem*

"Skinny-Dipping in Vathy" was recorded by Garrison Keillor as a featured poem for *The Writer's Almanac*

About the Author

Poet and writer **Barbara Quick** is best known as author of the internationally bestselling novel *Vivaldi's Virgins*, which has been translated into a dozen languages. Her first novel, *Northern Edge*, won the Discover: Great New Writers prize. Her fourth novel, *What Disappears*, is being launched by Regal House in 2022. Some of Barbara's poems have been recorded by Garrison Keillor and featured on *The Writer's Almanac*. She has been the featured guest on Grace Cavalieri's long-running program from the Library of Congress, "The Poet and the Poem." Barbara's essays, poems and book reviews have been published in many periodicals, including the *New York Times Book Review*, *Newsweek*, the *Annals of Internal Medicine*, the *Journal of Humanistic Mathematics*, the *San Francisco Chronicle*, *Canary*, the *Monterey Poetry Review* and other literary journals, both print and online. Her poems have been anthologized in *These Trees*, a large-format art book by photographer Ruthie Rosauer; *Fire and Rain: Ecopoetry of California* (co-edited by Lucille Lang Day and Ruth Nolan for Scarlet Tanager Books); *Fog and Light: San Francisco through the Eyes of the Poets Who Live Here* (Diane Frank, Editor, Blue Light Press); *Pandemic Puzzle Poems* (Diane Frank and Prartho Sereno, Editors, Blue Light Press). Based on a small farm and vineyard in the California Wine Country with her husband Wayne Roden, a vigneron and long-time violist with the San Francisco Symphony, Barbara takes Brazilian dance classes whenever possible.

More at BarbaraQuick.com

CPSIA information can be obtained
at www.ICGtesting.com
Printed in the USA
LVHW110913080521
686863LV00004B/288